OVERCOMING ADVERSITY:
SHARING THE AMERICAN DREAM

MARTIN LAWRENCE

MASON CREST PUBLISHERS
PHILADELPHIA

OVERCOMING ADVERSITY:
SHARING THE AMERICAN DREAM

OVERCOMING ADVERSITY:
SHARING THE AMERICAN DREAM

MARTIN LAWRENCE

STACIA DEUTSCH AND RHODY COHON

MASON CREST PUBLISHERS
PHILADELPHIA

ABOUT CROSS-CURRENTS

When you see this logo, turn to the Cross-Currents section at the back of the book. The Cross-Currents features explore connections between people, places, events, and ideas.

Produced by OTTN Publishing, Stockton, New Jersey

Mason Crest Publishers
370 Reed Road
Broomall, PA 19008
www.masoncrest.com

First printing

1 3 5 7 9 8 6 4 2

Library of Congress Cataloging-in-Publication Data

Deutsch, Stacia.
  Martin Lawrence / Stacia Deutsch, Rhody Cohon.
      p. cm. — (Sharing the American dream : overcoming adversity)
  Includes bibliographical references.
  ISBN 978-1-4222-0587-7 (hardcover) — ISBN 978-1-4222-0752-9 (pbk.)
  1. Lawrence, Martin, 1965- 2. Actors—United States—Biography—Juvenile literature. 3.
Comedians—United States—Biography—Juvenile literature. I. Cohon, Rhody. II. Title.
  PN2287.L28953D48 2009
  792.02'8092—dc22
  [B]
                              2008040024

OVERCOMING ADVERSITY:
SHARING THE AMERICAN DREAM

TABLE OF CONTENTS

CHAPTER ONE

IN HIS ELEMENT

On June 2, 2000, the wacky, action-packed comedy *Big Momma's House* opened in theaters throughout the United States. Its star and executive producer, Martin Lawrence, played a tough FBI agent and master of disguise, who must catch an escaped federal prisoner (played by Terrence Howard). To find out what the convict's ex-girlfriend (played by Nia Long) knows, the agent throws himself into his most challenging disguise yet: her outspoken, 300-pound grandmother. Things soon become complicated, especially when he finds himself falling for Big Momma's granddaughter—even as he suspects her of being a criminal.

The majority of critics didn't exactly love *Big Momma's House*, stressing its crude humor and its far-fetched plot. However, it seemed that the moviegoing public did. The film made $25 million in its opening weekend. It went on to be one of the big blockbusters of the summer of 2000, ultimately grossing nearly $120 million worldwide.

For Martin Lawrence, the success of *Big Momma's House* was especially meaningful. The gender-bending role had been challenging; to bring Big Momma to life, Lawrence had to wear a fat suit and spend two to three hours in a makeup chair for each day

A promotional picture from the movie *Big Momma's House*, a box-office hit in 2000. Its star, Martin Lawrence, worked out in order to portray a detective—and hid under layers of makeup and padding to create the detective's alter ego, Big Momma.

of filming. And to look convincing as the FBI agent, he had put his health in danger trying to lose weight. But Lawrence had already proved his ability to disguise his voice and appearance, in order to disappear into characters very different from himself (in fact, performing in women's clothing was one of his specialties). His hard work paid off, but more importantly, the movie's strong box office performance helped restore his professional reputation.

Starring in such a popular comedy indicated that Lawrence's career had recovered, after a long series of personal problems that had threatened to permanently overshadow his talent. Over the course of a few years, Lawrence had dealt with a messy divorce, run-ins with the law, a struggle with drug abuse, and frightening health emergencies. He was arrested several times. His behavior led to the cancellation of his television show—one of the most popular sitcoms of the 1990s, *Martin*, which had aired from 1992 to 1997. He gained a reputation for being difficult to work with, which may have cost him movie roles. To make matters worse, tabloid coverage had made all these incidents very public, and Lawrence became the subject of mockery and gossip.

In fact, the first time most people heard of *Big Momma's House* was in the context of rumors about Martin Lawrence. While Lawrence was shooting the movie, his attempt to lose weight took a very unhealthy turn. He became dangerously overheated while jogging and lapsed into a three-day coma. Lawrence recovered fully, but the experience frightened him, inspiring him to tackle his personal problems.

In 1997, at the height of Lawrence's personal and legal difficulties, a critic had speculated that Lawrence

READ MORE

In 1999, Martin Lawrence survived a coma and made a full recovery. To learn about the causes and effects of comas, turn to page 42.

Lawrence walks the red carpet at the May 31, 2000, premiere of *Big Momma's House*. Nia Long, who played his love interest in the movie, joins him.

was torn between being "a wiry, raunch-minded, fast-talking, off-kilter smartass, a little guy with a big mouth and a keen eye for a weak spot," and being "a ranting, incoherent menace...a basket case." *Big Momma's House* made many viewers enjoy seeing Lawrence as that funny, observant performer, and forget about the scandals that had surrounded him. The movie gave Lawrence the chance to show off the comedic skills that had made him famous. With his life seemingly back in order, Lawrence could focus on what he did best: making people laugh.

CHAPTER TWO

EARLY DAYS

Martin Fitzgerald Lawrence was born in Frankfurt, West Germany, on April 16, 1965. His mother, Chlora, named him after the renowned civil rights leader Martin Luther King, Jr. His middle name was given to him as a tribute to President John Fitzgerald Kennedy, who had been assassinated two years before Martin was born.

Martin's father, John Lawrence, served in the United States military in Germany. When Martin was seven, his family returned to the United States, settling in Landover, Maryland, near Washington, D.C. A year later, in 1973, Martin's parents divorced. Martin's mother had to struggle to provide for her six children, holding several cashier jobs in order to make ends meet. In a 1993 interview, Martin recalled cracking his first jokes, hoping to cheer his mother up when she returned from long days at work. "She'd come home from work tired," he said. "I would lie on the end of her bed, trying to make her laugh. I knew when I made my mother laugh, I had something."

Growing up, Martin was teased for being overweight. Some kids at school called him "Porker." During his teenage years, he took up boxing. In interviews, he makes light of his boxing skills, joking in 2005: "My coach had a good saying: 'One thing about

Martin, he ain't gonna get hit and he ain't gonna hit nobody!'" Despite what his modesty would suggest, he advanced to championship boxing matches in high school. He became a Mid-Atlantic Golden Gloves contender, and was a runner-up. Later, he also became an Amateur Athletic Union (AAU) champion. Boxing gave Martin a sense of self-confidence that he desperately needed. His boxing coach was like a father to him, and he credits boxing with keeping him busy after school and out of trouble.

A yearbook portrait of Martin Lawrence, the class clown of Eleanor Roosevelt High School in Greenbelt, Maryland. Martin realized at an early age how much he enjoyed telling jokes. He decided to do it for a living.

His First Comedy Routines

As much as Martin enjoyed boxing as a teen, his most distinctive talent proved to be comedy. Not only did he amuse his family by cracking jokes at home, but his antics soon spilled over into the classroom as well. The budding clown's routines disrupted the class so often that his art teacher made a deal with him, as he described in a 1999 interview:

> In high school, my art teacher finally said, "Martin, would you chill out! If you do, I'll give you the last five minutes of each day to do stand-up. But you have to be funny in order for me to say, 'class dismissed.'" It was my ultimate challenge.

He succeeded when he was able to make his fellow students laugh, and he was a hit in school. The art teacher gave Martin a business card from a local comedy club and suggested he check it out. Lawrence promised her that if he made it as a comedian, he'd buy her a car. (Eventually, he did.)

After graduating from high school in 1984, Lawrence decided to see if he could get the same response in local comedy clubs. He had hopes of fame and fortune, as he recalled in a 1999 interview: "I did dream all this good stuff would happen. The kid in you is always dreaming, 'I'm going to be a huge star.'"

The Underground Comedy Scene

Lawrence performed his stand-up act around Washington, D.C., in comedy clubs; but since that didn't pay well, he also worked as a janitor at a Kmart. He had some good performances and some that weren't so great, but Lawrence was determined to make a career for himself as a comedian. He has said that every performance helped him refine his skills.

Martin Lawrence has credited Richard Pryor—considered one of the best stand-up comedians of all time—with inspiring him in his early years as a performer. Pryor delivered his jokes as if he were telling stories, and was willing to turn even the most controversial topics, from racism to drug addiction, into punch lines. Lawrence wanted to follow in Pryor's footsteps, and similarly peppered his routines with stories about his own life and with vulgar, irreverent language.

When he felt he was ready for a city with a bigger comedy club circuit, Lawrence moved to New York City to try his luck as a comedian. He started out doing free shows in Washington Square Park.

READ MORE

Washington Square Park proved convenient for Martin Lawrence as he tried to get discovered. Check out page 43 to learn more about the New York City park.

Actor and stand-up comedian Richard Pryor in a 1987 photo. Martin Lawrence says that Pryor's comedy strongly influenced his own.

The crowded park had a built-in audience, making it a common starting place for aspiring actors, musicians, poets, and entertainers to try out material.

While in New York, Lawrence had some good opportunities to make a name for himself. In addition to his performances at the park, he also had some paying gigs. He performed at the Improv, a famous comedy club. Still, it was hard to make money doing stand-up, and Lawrence had to take additional jobs to pay his rent. For a while, he worked at a Sears department store in the city. Among his co-workers at Sears were other future entertainers: hip-hop/comedy duo Kid 'n' Play (who later appeared with Lawrence in several movies), and members of the rap group Salt-N-Pepa.

However, Lawrence didn't stay in New York City long. While working at a gas station, he was robbed at gunpoint. Shaken by the incident, he decided to return to Maryland and to the Washington, D.C., comedy clubs.

Appearing on *Star Search*

In 1987, Martin Lawrence auditioned to perform on TV's *Star Search*. The show was a reality-based contest between aspiring entertainers, much like today's *American Idol* and *America's Got Talent*. Lawrence's audition was successful; he was selected to compete in the comedy portion. He did well, winning one round; however, he didn't get the award in his category.

In a 1993 interview, Martin Lawrence remembered thinking that his appearance on *Star Search* was going to make him

READ MORE

Martin Lawrence isn't the only successful performer who competed on *Star Search*. See page 44 to learn more about the show.

famous. He had done well enough to assume that television executives would be calling at any minute. The phone didn't ring. Instead, Lawrence went back to his old janitor's job, cleaning floors. "I thought I'd made it!" he remembered later. "I had these pictures that I'd take out and show people and say, 'See, I was on *Star Search*,' and they'd say, 'If you was on *Star Search*, then what are you doing here?'"

Still, Lawrence continued to dream of fame, and then one day his phone really did ring. Executives at Columbia Pictures had seen a tape of Lawrence's *Star Search* performance. He was exactly what they were looking for. They offered Lawrence a recurring role on a television sitcom called *What's Happening Now!!*

Martin Lawrence performing at a West Hollywood comedy club in 2003. Although acting brought him more fame, he began his entertainment career as a stand-up comedian and has not abandoned this passion.

During the show's third and final season, from 1987 to 1988, Martin Lawrence played a quick-witted, smart-mouthed busboy. This was Lawrence's first regular television part, but it wouldn't be his last.

CHAPTER THREE

FROM SMALL-TIME TO PRIME TIME

Thanks to hard work spent building his reputation as a stand-up comedian in the comedy club circuit, Martin Lawrence found that opportunities to work on television and in the movies were coming his way.

During and after his time on *What's Happening Now!!*, Lawrence's popularity grew at comedy clubs. His stand-up material was quite different from what he had performed on *Star Search*. Lawrence's raunchy routines on race, sex, and life in general were definitely for mature audiences only. Those adult audiences found him funny. He was performing regularly at comedy clubs in Los Angeles, building a fan base, and finally making some money at the one job he wanted the most.

Lawrence's First Movie Roles

In 1989, Lawrence attracted the attention of movie director Spike Lee. In his acclaimed film *Do the Right Thing*, Lee cast Lawrence in a small but memorable part as a guy who buys a slice of pizza in the middle of a riot. Lawrence's brief appearance showed off his comic talent and attracted the attention of other filmmakers.

In 1990, Reginald and Warrington Hudlin cast Lawrence in their film *House Party*. Lawrence played a tone-deaf DJ

(From left to right) Martin Lawrence, Eddie Murphy, and David Alan Grier in a scene from the 1992 movie *Boomerang*. Murphy played a reformed womanizer, and Lawrence and Grier played his buddies.

spinning records at a party. His *House Party* co-stars included the rap duo Kid 'n' Play, whom he had befriended while they worked together at Sears in New York City. The *House Party* cast also included Tisha Campbell, who went on to collaborate with Lawrence a number of times, including on his television series.

The success of *House Party* led Martin Lawrence to appear in the sequel, *House Party 2*, in 1991. That same year, Lawrence also appeared in the gritty film *Talkin' Dirty After Dark*. It was his first starring role, but it was a small, independent movie that could not reach a wide audience. In 1992, Lawrence was offered a big role in the Hudlin brothers' next film, *Boomerang*, starring one of his favorite comedians, Eddie Murphy. Lawrence played one of Eddie Murphy's two closest

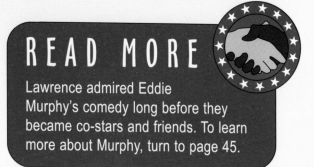

READ MORE

Lawrence admired Eddie Murphy's comedy long before they became co-stars and friends. To learn more about Murphy, turn to page 45.

friends. He has said that meeting Murphy for the first time left him stunned with excitement.

Becoming a Television Personality

All the while Lawrence was working on movie projects, he continued pursuing opportunities to take his act to television. In 1989, he appeared on *It's Showtime at the Apollo*, a late-night showcase for amateur and up-and-coming entertainers. Having attracted the attention of HBO executives, he was offered a half-hour special on the HBO series *One Night Stand* in 1991. The series featured stand-up comedy routines from some of the best comedians of the time, including such big names as Ellen DeGeneres, Bill Hicks, and George Wallace.

Lawrence's live performance on *One Night Stand* was widely acclaimed, by critics and the viewing public alike, and helped increase his profile. He was soon asked to be the host of another HBO series, *Russell Simmons' Def Comedy Jam*. *Def Comedy Jam* gave airtime only to America's best African-American stand-up comedians, such as Bernie Mac, Steve Harvey, and Chris Rock. *Def Comedy Jam* was the brainchild of music executive Russell Simmons, who reportedly hand-picked Martin Lawrence to host.

Lawrence hosted *Def Comedy Jam* for two seasons, which aired in 1992 and 1993. In each episode, he introduced each guest performer and did a little

READ MORE

To learn about Russell Simmons, the entertainment mogul who created *Def Comedy Jam*, turn to page 46.

stand-up of his own. Since the show aired on HBO, a cable channel as opposed to a network, he and the guests could use graphic language without any censoring. Lawrence took advantage of this setting, performing routines that were clearly just for adults.

Sitcom Stardom

Even as he hosted *Def Comedy Jam*, Lawrence was working on another project: his own, half-hour sitcom series, which would be aired on Fox. On August 27, 1992, the first episode of *Martin* aired.

Lawrence played the main character, Martin Payne, a stubborn, sarcastic young disc jockey and talk show host from Detroit. The sitcom revolved around Martin Payne's comic misadventures at work; with his family, friends, and neighbors; and in his relationship with his girlfriend. Lawrence incorporated material from his life and comedy routines into some story lines, and improvised much of his dialogue. The show was taped in front of a studio audience. As Sandy Grushow, president of Fox Entertainment Group, put it in 1993, *Martin* was "a fairly traditional sitcom" in terms of plot. What made *Martin* special, Grushow said, was its "talented cast headed by a young, loud, outrageous personality, Martin Lawrence."

READ MORE

For information about Fox, the television network that aired Martin Lawrence's sitcom, turn to page 47.

In addition to Lawrence, that cast included a number of other young actors and actresses, many of whom had previously worked together. Among them was Tisha Campbell, who had starred in the *House Party* movies with Lawrence. Campbell portrayed Martin's girlfriend, Gina, who becomes his wife. Other characters included Martin Payne's two best friends: Tommy Strawn, portrayed by Thomas Mikal Ford; and Cole Brown, played by Carl Anthony Payne II. Tichina Arnold took the role of Pamela James, Gina's best friend.

Tisha Campbell and Martin Lawrence in a promotional still from *Martin*. Many of the sitcom's story lines revolved around the unlikely romance between their characters—a successful businesswoman and a foulmouthed DJ.

In this scene from *Martin*, Lawrence (center) is decked out in women's clothing while still sporting a mustache. All the zany characters he played made the show distinctive and unpredictable.

A unique characteristic of *Martin* was the variety of roles played by Martin Lawrence himself—he portrayed many colorful supporting characters in addition to Martin Payne. Perhaps his most popular creation was Martin Payne's neighbor, loud-mouthed hairdresser Sheneneh Jenkins. At first the network didn't understand the character, but viewers loved her and she became a regular. Lawrence also played Martin Payne's overprotective mother, Mama Payne, modeling the character after his own mother and grandmother. Other audience favorites portrayed by Lawrence included womanizer Jerome; 10-year-old Roscoe (Lawrence walked on his knees to play him); washed-up musician Elroy; Bob, a white surfer dude; and Otis, an unstable security guard.

Not everyone enjoyed *Martin*; in fact, many people found it offensive. Well-known actor and comedian Bill Cosby expressed distaste for the show, stressing that he felt it reinforced negative stereotypes of black people. Others thought that the raunchy, often profane humor of *Martin* was inappropriate for its 8 P.M. time slot, when families were likely to be watching TV. But Lawrence said that the show's content was authentic, and that he would keep it that way—even as some Fox network executives worried that he would offend too many viewers.

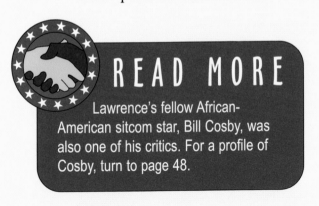

READ MORE

Lawrence's fellow African-American sitcom star, Bill Cosby, was also one of his critics. For a profile of Cosby, turn to page 48.

In 1994, Lawrence talked to *Entertainment Weekly* about the difficulties he encountered while incorporating questionable material into his show:

> I have to fight and fight to do the Martin show my way. You can't say this, you can't say that. ... [Fox Studios says:] "This is at 8 o'clock—what about the kids?" I'm like, "Hey, people know Martin. They ain't surprised...."

Despite the controversy surrounding *Martin*, the show was a big hit. High ratings eased the network's fear that the show was too profane, which eventually gave Lawrence more creative freedom. Many critics also approved of *Martin*. The show was awarded the NAACP (National Association for the Advancement of Colored People) Image Award in 1994 for Outstanding Television Series. It also won a People's Choice Award in 1993 for Favorite TV New Comedy Series. In addition, Lawrence himself won the NAACP Image Award in 1995 and 1996 for Outstanding Lead Actor in a Comedy Series.

CHAPTER FOUR

THE DANGERS OF FAME

By the mid-1990s, Martin Lawrence was a national celebrity. He was the star of a hit sitcom and of a growing number of movies. Television made Martin a household name. However, live stand-up comedy was his first love, and he continued to perform at clubs. That became a lucrative project, too. In 1993, Lawrence released a comedy album called *Martin Lawrence Live*. The album was on Billboard's chart for 33 weeks, reaching as high as number 10. Next came the 1994 concert film entitled *You So Crazy*. The movie captured Lawrence at his most vulgar and received an NC-17 rating. It was popular, however, and made a great deal of money.

To outside observers, Lawrence's personal life also seemed to be in great shape. On January 7, 1995, he married beauty queen Patricia Southall, first runner-up in the Miss USA 1994 pageant. Lawrence and Southall had met in 1992 at one of Lawrence's *Def Comedy Jam* shows. (Lawrence's previous engagement, to actress Lark Voorhies in 1993, had not worked out.) The lavish

READ MORE

For a profile of Patricia Southall, who married Martin Lawrence in 1995, turn to page 49.

Newlyweds Martin Lawrence and Patricia Southall arrive at the ShoWest Convention in September 1995. At the convention's award ceremony, Lawrence was named "Male Star of Tomorrow."

wedding took place in Southall's native Virginia with about 600 guests, including Eddie Murphy, Kid 'n' Play, and several cast members of *Martin*.

Lawrence may have appeared to be on top of the world, but in private, he was restless and on edge. It seemed to many who were close to him that the fame wasn't making him happy. "Success really just blew his mind the first year of [*Martin*]," a former Fox employee recalled to Allison Samuels of *Newsweek* in 1997. "Instead of being happy, he resented the people who put him there and became this power freak. As soon as success hit, he snapped." Samuels noted that Lawrence had unexpectedly fired his manager and *Martin* collaborator, Topper Carew, and started having frequent temper tantrums. All Lawrence said for himself was that he was overworked and stressed out, and that this stress "took its toll on everything around me."

It was unclear whether Lawrence's difficulties stemmed from being overworked, from anger at critics, or from paranoia over his sudden wealth. Lawrence seemed defensive about the criticism leveled against his show, and about the network's suggestions that he tone down its edgy, gritty humor. This manifested itself in what seemed to be increasingly frequent temper tantrums. Lawrence was also under stress from a busy schedule, and gained a reputation for difficult behavior on the set.

One of the first outward signs that Lawrence was having problems occurred in 1994. On February 19 he hosted an episode of the sketch comedy show *Saturday Night Live*, and was banned for life from the show for making explicit, unscripted comments during his opening monologue. Soon after, Lawrence's unpredictable antics began to occur more frequently. Eventually, he appeared to have lost control of himself.

Will Smith (right) teamed up with Martin Lawrence in the 1995 buddy film *Bad Boys*. Unfortunately for Lawrence, however, rumors about his personal life soon began to overshadow the movie's success.

Bizarre Behavior

Lawrence's personal issues did not immediately affect his movie career. In fact, in 1995, Lawrence appeared in one of his biggest hits yet, *Bad Boys*. He and Will Smith starred as mismatched detectives on a drug bust. The movie was a smash in theaters, and there were no reported incidents on the set. In fact,

READ MORE

To learn about the career of Will Smith, Lawrence's multi-talented *Bad Boys* co-star, turn to page 50.

producer Jerry Bruckheimer said later that Lawrence, along with Smith, consistently showed "ambition and energy as well as a genuine desire to please the audience, whatever it takes."

But it was also in 1995 that Lawrence had a very public, violent outburst while making another movie. His temper flared on the set of *A Thin Line Between Love and Hate*, which he wrote, produced, directed, and starred in. Cast and crew members of *Martin* also said that Lawrence had been behaving oddly and unpleasantly, often screaming at people. Rumors soon flew that he was on illegal drugs. At the very least—according to Lawrence's wife—as of summer 1995, he was taking prescribed psychiatric drugs.

One day in May 1996, on the set of the movie *Nothing to Lose*, Lawrence was laughing hysterically for no apparent reason and messing up his lines. The director, Steve Oedekerk, sent Lawrence home. But Lawrence's wife said that he did not come home until 5 A.M. A few hours later, Lawrence wandered back outside and into a busy intersection on Ventura Boulevard in Los Angeles. Police found him screaming at cars, with a gun in his pocket.

The police took Lawrence straight to Cedars-Sinai Medical Center. The hospital ran blood tests to determine if there were drugs or alcohol in his system at the time of the incident. Lawrence admitted that he had been smoking marijuana, and a hospital spokesperson told reporters that Lawrence had suffered a seizure as a result of prescription medication. But the doctor who performed drug tests on Lawrence said there had been no seizure, and Lawrence had no drugs, prescribed or otherwise, in his system. Lawrence's spokespeople said he was dehydrated and exhausted. The incident was a news sensation, but ultimately, the public had no logical explanation for what had caused it.

Martin Lawrence and Patricia Southall at the Los Angeles premiere of *A Thin Line Between Love and Hate*, in April 1996. The couple divorced later that year.

Lawrence returned to the set of *Nothing to Lose* two days after his arrest and hospitalization, and the movie was eventually successful. He also hired a private nurse to live with him and manage his stress and medications. But the outbursts did not end there.

Legal Problems

As these strange incidents were piling up, Lawrence's marriage was also in trouble. In September 1996, less than two years after they were married, Martin Lawrence and Patricia Southall were divorced. Southall then filed a restraining order against Lawrence, claiming that she feared for her safety and the safety of their baby daughter, Jasmine Page, who was born on January 15, 1996. The restraining order prohibited Lawrence from going near Southall or their daughter. Southall said in court documents that Lawrence's behavior had become unpredictable, aggressive, and frightening. She claimed he picked fights, made verbal threats, and had hit her at least once. When requesting the restraining order, Southall stated: "Sometimes Petitioner [Lawrence] is himself and sometimes he is not. I can never be sure."

In January 1997, Lawrence's *Martin* co-star Tisha Campbell filed a lawsuit against the actor, accusing him of sexual harassment and battery. Campbell claimed that Lawrence's inappropriate behavior, which included slapping her, had made her afraid to be anywhere near him. After the lawsuit was settled out of court (the terms of settlement were kept private), Fox executives convinced Campbell to finish what had to be the final season of *Martin*. But she was only willing to return if she never had to interact with Lawrence. The show's writers had to come up with ways to make the characters Martin and Gina seem like a happy couple without ever appearing on-screen together. For example, Gina started taking frequent business trips, and she and Martin

CHAPTER FIVE

MOVING FORWARD

Martin Lawrence had undergone a divorce and a series of legal problems. He had even survived a coma. The traumas inspired him to give up drug use and reevaluate his career. He didn't want to give up acting, but he did think he needed more time to himself. Lawrence told Tavis Smiley of PBS:

> I just ain't had nothing to say. I was too busy try-ing to get me together. Me in order. I had so many things going on in my life. So, I had to get me in order before I could get out and talk about anything, you know what I mean? So, I took time off. . . . I just had to take the time to myself.

In the same interview, Smiley asked Lawrence what had helped him survive that very difficult period of his life. Lawrence replied:

> First and foremost, my God. My faith and my belief. My family, my friends, truly were there with me every step of the way. When times were hard, I wasn't believing in this or believing in that, or

getting in this, getting in that, they stuck with me all the way. And no matter what all the negative things that was being said about me, a much greater force was working in my life, which was my God.

Mixed Success

Even as Lawrence tried to relax and make time for himself, he did not stop working. He starred in two movies in 1999. First he reunited with Eddie Murphy for the movie *Life*, in which

READ MORE

Martin Lawrence grants fewer interviews than he used to. To learn about Tavis Smiley, one media figure he has spoken with, turn to page 51.

they both played wrongly convicted prisoners. Then Lawrence portrayed a diamond thief pretending to be a cop in a film entitled *Blue Streak*. Neither movie was a box-office smash, but

Martin Lawrence and Luke Wilson in *Blue Streak*, which premiered less than a month after Lawrence's coma. Although Lawrence realized he needed a less hectic schedule, he resumed promotional work for *Blue Streak* as soon as he left the hospital.

Old and New Roles

Since the end of *Martin*, Lawrence has not pursued further work in television acting, although he did produce a stand-up comedy showcase, *Martin Lawrence Presents: 1st Amendment Stand-Up*,

Lawrence greets onlookers at the Hollywood premiere of *College Road Trip* on March 3, 2008. His venture into kids' movies, like *College Road Trip*, surprised fans and critics.

getting in this, getting in that, they stuck with me all the way. And no matter what all the negative things that was being said about me, a much greater force was working in my life, which was my God.

Mixed Success

Even as Lawrence tried to relax and make time for himself, he did not stop working. He starred in two movies in 1999. First he reunited with Eddie Murphy for the movie *Life*, in which

READ MORE

Martin Lawrence grants fewer interviews than he used to. To learn about Tavis Smiley, one media figure he has spoken with, turn to page 51.

they both played wrongly convicted prisoners. Then Lawrence portrayed a diamond thief pretending to be a cop in a film entitled *Blue Streak*. Neither movie was a box-office smash, but

Martin Lawrence and Luke Wilson in *Blue Streak*, which premiered less than a month after Lawrence's coma. Although Lawrence realized he needed a less hectic schedule, he resumed promotional work for *Blue Streak* as soon as he left the hospital.

Martin Lawrence Live: Runteldat was Lawrence's first stand-up film since 1994. Throughout the movie, Lawrence (seen here at its Hollywood premiere on July 29, 2002) turns his personal problems into jokes.

many critics found *Life* interesting and praised the ability of Murphy and Lawrence to convincingly play much older men (the movie spanned more than 50 years in the characters' lives).

Big Momma's House was the first blockbuster after Lawrence's coma in which he was the only lead. His two movies released in 2001 were not nearly as successful, however. *What's the*

Worst that Could Happen? and *Black Knight* were both easily forgotten, and Lawrence continued to search for new projects that would have the same kind of success he'd found with *Big Momma's House*.

A Healing Experience

As Lawrence continued acting in movies, he also returned to his roots and embarked on a national stand-up tour in 2001. In 2002, he released a new stand-up comedy film, taped in Washington, D.C., called *Martin Lawrence Live: Runteldat*. The movie was his visual autobiography, allowing him to laugh at and make fun of the hardships he had been through.

The movie began with a short montage about all the things that Lawrence had experienced, laying out a full picture of his poor behavior. He acknowledged that he had made a lot of mistakes—but he also made it clear that he would not ignore what critics and tabloids were saying about him. (The movie's subtitle was short for "run and tell that," implying that Lawrence thought the media was too eager to spread gossip.) Then, he launched into a stand-up routine. It was his chance to explain what had happened to him from his perspective, and to do it in a very funny way.

In an interview just prior to the release of *Runteldat*, Lawrence described making the film as painful, but ultimately rewarding:

> It was difficult in the sense that I had to go back and relive it. It's one thing to go through everything I've been through and then get past it and move on. But to do standup and get out the paper clippings and news reports of yourself, it's a hard thing to go through but very therapeutic for me, because it reminded me and gave me some understanding. It humbled me to a degree to say, wow, that was me.

Old and New Roles

Since the end of *Martin*, Lawrence has not pursued further work in television acting, although he did produce a stand-up comedy showcase, *Martin Lawrence Presents: 1st Amendment Stand-Up,*

Lawrence greets onlookers at the Hollywood premiere of *College Road Trip* on March 3, 2008. His venture into kids' movies, like *College Road Trip*, surprised fans and critics.

in 2007. He retired his sitcom's characters, preferring not to create any spin-off shows for them or see them appear anywhere else. So far, the only time he has revisited any of his *Martin* roles was in 2006, during a television interview on *Inside the Actors Studio*. Without a script or costumes, simply sitting in his chair, Lawrence re-created the voices of several characters. The studio audience was thrilled.

Many of Lawrence's recent movie projects have been sequels to his biggest hits. In 2003, Lawrence teamed up with Will Smith again to star in *Bad Boys II*. It was even more successful than the first *Bad Boys* movie at the box office. And in 2006, he starred in *Big Momma's House 2*. Nia Long, who played his love interest in *Big Momma's House*, also returned. Like its predecessor, *Big Momma's House 2* was very profitable at the box office, although most of its reviews were not positive.

Aside from sequels, several of Lawrence's recent films have appealed to a younger audience. In 2005, Lawrence starred alongside teen actors in the film *Rebound*. The movie was a good fit for Lawrence—he portrayed a basketball coach with a bad temper who is looking for a second chance. Lawrence tried his hand at voice acting in 2006, playing a grizzly bear named Boog in the children's animated comedy *Open Season*. In 2008, he appeared in another family-friendly movie, *College Road Trip*, as the overprotective father of a teenage girl.

Lawrence is often asked why many of his newer projects are family-friendly, compared to the gritty work that made him famous. Lawrence says he started tackling such roles because of his own children. He and his companion, Shamicka Gibbs (they are now reportedly married), have two daughters: Iyanna, born in 2001, and Amara, born in 2003. They joined Lawrence's daughter, Jasmine, from his marriage to Patricia Southall. "Kids made the difference," Lawrence has explained about his decision to be in family movies. "In my body of work, I want to do things that my kids can enjoy as well."

Lawrence still makes movies that adults would enjoy, however. He starred in another buddy-cop movie in 2003, called *National Security*. In 2007's *Wild Hogs*, Lawrence played one of four friends on a road trip that takes unexpected turns. And in *Welcome Home Roscoe Jenkins* (2008), Lawrence's character is a famous talk show host who realizes the importance of family when he visits his hometown. These movies were packed with Lawrence's signature screwball comedy. Confident that he can appeal to both young and adult viewers, he remarked in 2008: "[W]hether I'm being edgy or clean, I like to think that I'm likable, no matter what I'm doing. My adult audience has kids, so there's a little something for everyone."

A reporter asked the writer-director of *Welcome Home Roscoe Jenkins*, Malcolm D. Lee, if there had been any problems working with Lawrence. Lee's reply indicated that Lawrence's behavior on the set did not reflect his troubled past:

> I love Martin. He's one of the most professional people I've ever worked with. He was always on time, always knew his lines, he was really there for the other actors. He empowered me right off the bat, told me, "You're the boss and the director." He dubbed me "Coach."

Future Plans

Despite his past behavior, Martin Lawrence has been able to reestablish himself as a highly respected, hardworking, and widely sought-after actor in Hollywood. Lawrence earned $20 million for starring in *Bad Boys II* in 2003, and has topped $10 million per film since then. This star power seems certain to lend itself to further success.

Martin Lawrence with Mo'Nique in a scene from *Welcome Home Roscoe Jenkins* (2008).

Martin Lawrence has succeeded in movies, television, and stand-up comedy, thanks to hard work and the ability to amuse his viewers.

Lawrence's future movie projects seem likely to revisit his most popular roles. Will Smith, his co-star in *Bad Boys* and *Bad Boys II*, has reportedly expressed interest in a third installment, and so has the series director, Michael Bay. In 2008, an *Open Season* sequel and a third *Big Momma's House* movie were also reported to be in early stages of development.

Whatever Martin Lawrence decides to do next, it's a safe bet that he will continue to leave audiences laughing. And, as he said in 2008, he isn't finished challenging himself to play new kinds of roles:

> I don't think I've gotten everything because all of the work that you've seen that I've done—I feel like the best is yet to come. . . . I might have just started scratching the surface. I don't believe you've seen everything that I'm capable of.

CROSS-CURRENTS

Comas

The word *coma* comes from a Greek word that means "deep sleep." It refers to the state of being deeply unconscious. Being in a coma, or comatose, is different from being asleep. A comatose patient cannot be awakened. His or her body won't respond normally to pain, to noise, or to light. A comatose person appears totally unresponsive.

If a person goes into a coma, it is usually because of some kind of abnormality in the body, such as a clogged kidney as a result of diabetes; or a disease, like meningitis. Comas may also be due to a heart attack, a stroke or seizure, or a head injury. Sometimes people lapse into comas after inhaling carbon monoxide or nearly drowning. Occasionally, doctors give patients drugs to induce comas; reducing blood flow to the brain can prevent the brain from swelling as a result of an injury or surgery.

Most comatose patients eventually regain consciousness between a few days and a few weeks (however, some patients die or remain comatose for years). Some people who wake up from comas find that they can return to their lives after a short rehabilitation period, with little permanent damage to the brain or to other important bodily functions. Others may never fully recover.

A comatose person cannot respond normally to being touched, and may still behave unpredictably after waking up. Some patients (such as Martin Lawrence) heal quickly, while others suffer permanent brain damage.

Washington Square Park

New York City residents and tourists alike enjoy Washington Square Park. The park is located at the lower end of Fifth Avenue in Greenwich Village. Since its early beginnings in 1826, this park has been used as both a cultural center and a casual meeting place.

A well-known attraction, the park is easily recognizable for its ornate sculptural features. A fountain, constructed in 1872, is a popular place for swimmers. In 1889, the park added a large archway to commemorate the 100-year anniversary of George Washington's inauguration as president of the United States. Later, in 1892, it was remade from marble. There is an inscription inside the arch which repeats Washington's words: "Let us raise a standard to which the wise and the honest can repair. The event is in the hand of God." Statues in the park include those depicting Italian patriot and soldier Giuseppe Garibaldi, and engineer Alexander Lyman Holley.

Today, most of the buildings around the park belong to New York University, and the university's graduation ceremony is held in the park each spring. The park also has a long-standing reputation as a place where street performers come to show off their music, comedy, magic tricks, or other forms of entertainment.

A calm day in New York City's Washington Square Park. The elaborate, marble arch is probably the park's most recognizable feature.

Star Search

Star Search was a talent competition that aired on television from 1983 through 1995. It was hosted by Ed McMahon. The show's contestants competed in a wide variety of talent categories, including Male Vocalist, Female Vocalist, Junior Vocalist, Vocal Group, Spokesperson, and Comedy.

Aspiring talents had to audition to appear on the show, and then two contestants went head-to-head in each category. The judges awarded each act one to five stars, which were averaged to determine the winner. In the event of a tie, the studio audience was allowed to vote and declare the winner.

In 2003, a new version of *Star Search* appeared on television, hosted by Arsenio Hall. It ran for two years on CBS. However, the similar *American Idol*, which had debuted in 2002, was more popular, and *Star Search* was ultimately canceled.

No recording or television contract was guaranteed; winners received cash prizes. For many *Star Search* competitors, appearing on TV was the real reward. Many famous people got their start on *Star Search*, though not always as the winners. In addition to Martin Lawrence, performers who competed on *Star Search* include Britney Spears, Jessica Simpson, Dave Chappelle, Lisa Tucker, Justin Timberlake, Sharon Stone, Ray Romano, Rosie O'Donnell, Dennis Miller, Drew Carey, and Alanis Morissette.

Pop singer Christina Aguilera is just one of many entertainers who competed on *Star Search* and went on to achieve fame.

Eddie Murphy

Edward Regan "Eddie" Murphy is an actor, producer, and stand-up comedian. Born in 1961 in Brooklyn, New York, Murphy has performed in more than 33 movies.

Murphy first became a household name as a regular cast member of NBC's *Saturday Night Live* from 1980 to 1984. In 1982, while still performing on *Saturday Night Live*, he made the transition to movies with a supporting role in *48 Hours*, starring Nick Nolte. Murphy soon won lead roles in a variety of blockbuster comedies, including *Trading Places*, *Beverly Hills Cop I* and *II*, and *Coming to America*.

Murphy received Golden Globe award nominations for his roles in *Beverly Hills Cop*, *Trading Places*, and *The Nutty Professor*. In 2007, Murphy finally won a Golden Globe, for his acting and singing role in the movie *Dreamgirls*. That performance also earned him an Academy Award nomination for Best Supporting Actor.

Eddie Murphy's humor appeals to two very different audiences. His stand-up comedy routines are definitely for adults, and so are many of his movies, including *Coming to America* and the *Beverly Hills Cop* series. But he has also starred in family-friendly hits, such as *Daddy Day Care*, *The Haunted Mansion*, and *Dr. Dolittle*. In fact, his best-known roles include voice work in animated movies for children. Murphy voiced the dragon Mushu in *Mulan*, and Donkey in all of the *Shrek* movies.

Eddie Murphy and his young co-star, Khamani Griffin, in a scene from *Daddy Day Care*. The kid-friendly comedy film was released in 2003.

CROSS-CURRENTS

Russell Simmons

A multimedia success, Russell Simmons is fondly thought of as a founding father of hip-hop music. He began his career as a producer, managing the rapper Kurtis Blow, the band Run-DMC, and the band the Beastie Boys. By 1984, he had founded his own recording company, Def Jam Recordings. He and his partner, Frederick "Rick" Rubin, played a big role in making hip-hop popular.

Simmons is also an influential figure in the fashion world. In 1982, he created a clothing line for men called Phat Farm. He also aided in the 1998 creation of Baby Phat, a women's fashion line designed by his wife. In 2004, Simmons sold Phat Farm for $140 million.

Clothing and music aren't the only places that Simmons made his mark. He has also opened his own movie production studio, developed television shows such as HBO's *Russell Simmons' Def Comedy Jam*, published a magazine, and built his own advertising agency.

Simmons shares his wealth by contributing to many charitable causes. He is the head of Rush Philanthropic Arts Foundation, an organization that gives underprivileged youth access to art and music. Simmons has also served on the board of the Foundation for Ethnic Understanding, which helps bring people of different religions and ethnicities together.

Russell Simmons (right) and model Heidi Albertsen in New York City, November 12, 2008, co-hosting a charity fund-raiser to help children in Tanzania. Simmons lends his support to numerous children's causes.

Fox Television Network

In 1985, the movie studio 20th Century Fox announced plans to form an independent television system. At the time, there were three main TV networks in the United States: CBS, NBC, and ABC. The owner of Fox Studios, Rupert Murdoch, declared that there would be no limits to what Fox Studios would put on television.

To compete with the older networks, Murdoch wanted edgy material that would attract viewers between the ages of 18 and 49. In April 1987, Fox premiered a comedy called *Married...with Children*. The show became a megahit, remaining on the air for 11 seasons.

The Tracey Ullman Show also debuted in 1987. The sketch comedy show ran for four seasons, but it is best known for the 30-second animated clips shown before and after commercial breaks. In 1989, Fox created *The Simpsons*, a spin-off based on those clips. *The Simpsons* became the longest-running sitcom and animated series of all time.

Another contribution the Fox network has made to popular culture is through interactive reality programming. *America's Most Wanted*, which premiered in 1988, profiles fugitives in the hope that viewers can help find them. The talent contest *American Idol* debuted in 2002 and quickly became one of the most popular reality shows yet, launching the careers of a number of singers.

These plush toys depict Homer and Bart Simpson, characters in the iconic cartoon *The Simpsons*. Since its 1989 debut, *The Simpsons* has been a huge hit for the Fox television network.

Bill Cosby

Bill Cosby started his career in entertainment as a stand-up comedian, performing in comedy clubs. In 1965, Cosby made headlines when he costarred with Robert Culp in the television show *I Spy*—he was the first African American to star in a dramatic television series.

Following *I Spy*, he focused his attention on children's programming. Cosby was the creator and host of an animated show called *Fat Albert and the Cosby Kids*. The show was based on his own childhood and ran from 1972 to 1979 and then was renewed from 1979 till 1984 under the new title *The New Fat Albert and the Cosby Kids*. Using the show as a tool for educators, Cosby wrote about the show for his own doctoral thesis. He received a Ph.D. in Education in 1977.

In 1984, Cosby both produced and starred in another landmark television series. *The Cosby Show* portrayed the life of an upper-middle-class African American family. The popular sitcom ran until 1992.

In 1999, Cosby developed yet another hit television show. *Little Bill*, a program aimed at preschoolers, was created for Nickelodeon. Today Bill Cosby is well known as a comedian, actor, producer, and director, but perhaps most importantly as an educator and role model.

Bill Cosby hosts a March 2008 celebration for the Jackie Robinson Foundation, a scholarship program. A longtime advocate for education, Cosby often says that entertainers have a responsibility to use their fame positively.

Patricia Southall

Patricia Annette Southall was born in 1971. A native of Chesapeake, Virginia, she graduated from James Madison University with a degree in journalism. In 1993, Southall won the Miss Virginia USA beauty pageant. She went on to represent Virginia in the 1994 Miss USA competition. She won the swimsuit competition and did well in her preliminary interview. She was also named "Most Photogenic" by the pageant's press. Southall didn't win the overall competition, but she finished as the first runner-up to Lu Parker of South Carolina.

Southall met Martin Lawrence in 1992 while she was working in the media office of Governor L. Douglas Wilder in Richmond, Virginia. Lawrence had come to Virginia to perform with the tour of HBO's *Russell Simmons' Def Comedy Jam*. The two married in 1995, but divorced in 1996. During their short marriage, they had a daughter together: Jasmine Page Lawrence.

In 2000, Southall remarried. This time she wed professional football player and *Dancing with the Stars* champion Emmitt Smith. They have a son named Emmitt IV. Southall is also stepmom to Smith's daughter, Regan.

Patricia Southall accompanies her husband, retired running back Emmitt Smith, at the 8th Annual Family Television Awards on November 29, 2006.

Will Smith

Willard Christopher "Will" Smith Jr. was born on September 25, 1968, and was raised in and around Philadelphia, Pennsylvania. A well-liked entertainer, he has achieved success in music, movies, and television.

Smith first got noticed in the late 1980s, as vocalist of the rap duo DJ Jazzy Jeff & The Fresh Prince. With a couple of major hit songs, especially "Parents Just Don't Understand" and "Summertime," the duo helped bring rap music to the mainstream. In 1989, "Parents Just Don't Understand" won the first Grammy Award given to a rap song.

In 1990, Smith made his acting debut on *The Fresh Prince of Bel-Air*, an NBC sitcom created just for him. The show became a big hit, running for six seasons until 1996. After Smith's successful transition from music to television, he branched out to movies. Supporting roles in *Made in America* and *Six Degrees of Separation* set the stage for his first megahit, *Bad Boys*, alongside Martin Lawrence. Since then, Will Smith has starred in a long parade of blockbuster films, such as *Independence Day* (1996), *Men in Black* (1997), *Enemy of the State* (1998), *Ali* (2001), *I, Robot* (2004), *Hitch* (2005), *The Pursuit of Happyness* (2006), and the sequels to *Men in Black* and *Bad Boys*. His most recent films include *I Am Legend* (2007) and *Hancock* (2008).

Will Smith attends the London premiere of his science fiction film *I Am Legend*, on December 19, 2007.

Tavis Smiley

Tavis Smiley is a journalist, political commentator, talk show host, and author. Born in 1964 in Gulfport, Mississippi, Smiley was raised primarily near Peru, Indiana. He attended Indiana University, where he studied public affairs and became active in local politics. After graduation, he worked as an aide to Tom Bradley, the mayor of Los Angeles. In 1991, Smiley ran unsuccessfully for Los Angeles City Council.

Smiley then turned his attention to radio and became a broadcaster. He did a series of one-minute reports called *The Smiley Report* for a Los Angeles-based station. *The Smiley Report* focused on local and national current-affairs issues affecting the African-American community. Smiley's commentary became popular, and *The Smiley Report* eventually expanded to a national audience.

In 1996, Smiley started commenting regularly on the *Tom Joyner Morning Show*, a national radio program. This national radio show gave Smiley exposure, and his popularity increased. He hosted *The Tavis Smiley Show* on National Public Radio from 2002 to 2004; the show is now aired by Public Radio International. Smiley also hosts a talk show on public television.

Tavis Smiley hosts an annual political summit, State of the Black Union, and was the moderator for two 2007 presidential debates. He has written and edited several books.

Tavis Smiley celebrates the thousandth episode of his talk show on September 18, 2008. According to Smiley, the key to a successful interview is to make the subject feel comfortable.

Chronology

1965: Martin Fitzgerald Lawrence born on April 16 in Frankfurt, West Germany.

1972: Moves with family to Landover, Maryland.

1973: Parents divorce.

1984: Graduates from high school in Maryland; begins performing stand-up comedy at clubs in the Washington, D.C., area.

1987: Competes on *Star Search*. Cast in recurring role on *What's Happening Now!!* in its third and final season.

1989: Appears in his first motion picture role, in Spike Lee's *Do the Right Thing*.

1990: Appears in the Hudlin brothers' movie *House Party*, starring friends Kid 'n' Play.

1992: Hosts *Russell Simmons' Def Comedy Jam* for first of two seasons; begins a five-year run of sitcom *Martin*.

1993: Releases first concert album.

1994: Hosts *Saturday Night Live*; is banned from the show after delivering a controversial opening monologue. First concert film, *You So Crazy*, is released and receives an NC-17 rating.

1995: Marries Patricia Southall; has an outburst on the set of the film *A Thin Line Between Love and Hate*.

1996: Daughter, Jasmine Page, is born. Under negative circumstances, gets divorced from his wife. Arrested in Los Angeles for waving a pistol and shouting at passing cars. Accused of sexual harassment by *Martin* co-star Tisha Campbell.

1999: Lapses into a three-day coma upon collapsing after a run.

2000: Stars in *Big Momma's House*.

2001: Daughter Iyanna is born.

2002: Releases a new concert film titled *Martin Lawrence Live: Runteldat*.

2003: Daughter Amara is born; stars in *Bad Boys II*.

2006: Lends his voice to animated movie *Open Season*; stars in *Big Momma's House 2*.

2007: Stars in *Wild Hogs*.

2008: Stars in two comedy movies: *College Road Trip* and *Welcome Home Roscoe Jenkins*.

Accomplishments/Awards
Awards

1993 People's Choice Award for Favorite TV New Comedy Series [For *Martin*]
1994 NAACP Image Award for Outstanding Television Series [For *Martin*]
1995 NAACP Image Award for Outstanding Lead Actor in a Comedy Series
1996 NAACP Image Award for Outstanding Lead Actor in a Comedy Series
2005 BET Icon Comedy Award

Movies

Do the Right Thing, 1989

House Party, 1990

Talkin' Dirty After Dark, 1991

House Party 2, 1991

Boomerang, 1992

Bad Boys, 1995

A Thin Line Between Love and Hate, 1996

Nothing to Lose, 1997

Life, 1999

Blue Streak, 1999

Big Momma's House, 2000

What's the Worst That Could Happen?, 2001

Black Knight, 2001

National Security, 2003

Bad Boys II, 2003

Rebound, 2005

Big Momma's House 2, 2006

Open Season, 2006

Wild Hogs, 2007

Welcome Home Roscoe Jenkins, 2008

College Road Trip, 2008

Television

What's Happening Now!!, 1987–1988

Russell Simmons' Def Comedy Jam, 1992–1993

Martin, 1992–1997

Albums and Concert Films

Martin Lawrence Live, 1993

You So Crazy, 1994

Martin Lawrence Live: Runteldat, 2002

Further Reading

Ascher-Walsh, Rebecca. "The Martin Chronicles." *Entertainment Weekly.* http://www.ew.com/ew/article/0,,256123,00.html

Hornaday, Ann. "Martin Lawrence, Still So Crazy." *Washington Post* (August 2, 2002).

Mcguigan, Cathleen. "Newsmakers." *Newsweek* (August 12, 2002).

Moss, Robert F. "The Shrinking Life Span of the Black Sitcom." *New York Times* (February 25, 2001).

Turner, Miki. "Martin Lawrence Is Comedy's Original Gangster." http://www.msnbc.msn.com/id/23452641/ (March 3, 2008).

Internet Resources

http://www.tv.com/martin/show/336/summary.html

This Web site contains information about the *Martin* television show, including a list of episodes.

http://us.imdb.com/name/nm0001454/bio

The Internet Movie Database Web site's page on Lawrence has a biography, a list of his award nominations, and an extensive list of his television and movie appearances and albums.

http://movies.yahoo.com/movie/contributor/1800018735/bio

The Yahoo! Movies page on Martin Lawrence includes a short biography, a milestones section, and more.

http://www.pbs.org/kcet/tavissmiley/archive/200601/2006 0125_lawrence.html

The *Tavis Smiley Show* Web site includes the transcript of an extensive interview conducted with Lawrence and a link to replay the show.

http://teacher.scholastic.com/scholasticnews/indepth/ rebound.asp

This Web site includes a special *Scholastic News* interview with Martin Lawrence.

Glossary

aspiring—striving toward a goal.

autobiography—a work that a person creates about his or her own life.

comedy club—a place where comedians perform in front of a live audience.

gigs—commitments by an entertainer for particular performances.

NC-17—a rating on a movie that declares that no one under the age of 17 will be allowed to view that movie in theaters.

rap—rhythmic, spoken word that is set to music, typically with a steady beat.

raunchy—sexually suggestive.

rehabilitation—therapy or education meant to restore a person to good health.

restraining order—a legal document that blocks access to one person by another.

sitcom—a plot-based, mostly comedic television show (short for "situation comedy").

stereotypes—oversimplified images of others.

womanizer—a person who pursues women in a degrading manner.

Chapter Notes

p. 9: "a wiry, raunch-minded . . ." Sharon Waxman, "The Tragedy of the Comic." *Washington Post*, June 24, 1997. http://www.washingtonpost.com/wp-srv/style/longterm/movies/review97/fmartinlawrence.htm

p. 10: "She'd come home . . ." Tim Allis, "Court Jester," *People*, April 12, 1993. http://www.people.com/people/archive/article/0,,20122118,00.html

p. 10: "My coach had a good . . ." "Martin Lawrence— Lawrence's Questionable Boxing Skills," http://www.contactmusic.com, June 22, 2005. http://www.contactmusic.com/new/xmlfeed.nsf/mndwebpages/lawrences%20questionable%20boxing%20skills

p. 11: "In high school . . ." Cindy Pearlman, "Battling the Blues, Lawrence Leaving Troubles Behind," *Chicago-Sun Times*, September 14, 1999, p. 36.

p. 12: "I did dream all..." Pearlman, "Battling the Blues."

p. 15: "I thought I'd made..." Allis, "Court Jester."

p. 19: "a fairly traditional..." Bill Carter, "The Networks' Best Laid Plans," *New York Times*, April 4, 1999.

p. 22: "I have to fight..." "Does Martin Have Legs?" *Entertainment Weekly*, February 4, 1994. http://www.ew.com/ew/article/0,,301028,00.html

p. 25: "Success really just…" Allison Samuels, "A Comic's Erratic Ride," *Newsweek*, July 21, 1997. http://www.newsweek.com/id/97942?tid=relatedcl

p. 25: "took its toll…" Samuels, "A Comic's Erratic Ride."

p. 27: "ambition and energy…" Nicole Walker, "Martin Lawrence and Will Smith Are Back in *Bad Boys II*," *Jet*, July 21, 2003. http://findarticles.com/p/articles/mi_m1355/is_4_104/ai_105619361

p. 29: "Sometimes Petitioner [Lawrence]…" Waxman, "The Tragedy of the Comic."

p. 30: "It's been bittersweet …" Samuels, "A Comic's Erratic Ride."

p. 31: "Your functions…" "Near Death Experience Gives Lawrence Wake-Up Call," February 25, 2000. http://archives.cnn.com/2000/SHOWBIZ/News/02/25/showbuzz/

p. 31: "It kind of…" Steve Ryfle, "Newsmakers: Martin Lawrence 'Just Happy to Be Here'," February 25, 2000. http://www.hollywood.com

p. 32: "I just ain't had…" Tavis Smiley, "Martin Lawrence," *The Tavis Smiley Show*, January 25, 2006. http://www.pbs.org/kcet/tavissmiley/archive/200601/20060125.html

p. 32: "First and foremost…" Smiley, "Martin Lawrence."

p. 35: "It was difficult…" Wilson Morales, "Still Going Strong!" August 2002. http://www.blackfilm.com/20020802/features/martinlawrence.shtml

p. 37: "Kids made the…" Greg Braxton, "Welcome Home, Martin," *Los Angeles Times*, February 7, 2008. http://articles.latimes.com/2008/feb/07/entertainment/et-martin7

p. 38: "[W]hether I'm being..." Braxton, "Welcome Home, Martin."

p. 38: "I love Martin..." Braxton, "Welcome Home, Martin."

p. 41: "I don't think..." Miki Turner, "Martin Lawrence Is Comedy's Original Gangster," March 3, 2008. http://www.msnbc.msn.com/id/23452641/

Index

Numbers in **bold italics** refer to captions.

Photo Credits

About the Authors

STACIA DEUTSCH AND RHODY COHON have written more than 21 books in the past four years. Stacia lives in Irvine, California, with her three children. Rhody lives in Tucson, Arizona, with her three kids.